Popular Canadian Curriculum Series

Canadian Curriculum

SummerSmart

English • Math • Science • Social Studies

Grades
K·1

Credits

Photo (Cover "children" famveldman/123RF.com)

Printed in China

ISBN: 978-1-77149-276-8

English

Mathematics

Science

Social Studies

Arts & Crafts

Contents

Grades K-1

Week

Week

Dear Parent:

While all work and no play makes Jack a dull boy, all play and no work would probably make Jack forget most of what he has learned, which is why it is necessary to schedule regular practice in the long summer vacation to help your child consolidate what he or she has learned.

This is where Canadian Curriculum SummerSmart can help.

Canadian Curriculum SummerSmart provides practice for your child to review the essentials taught in the previous academic year and prepares him or her for the grade ahead with confidence. The series is organized in an easy-to-use format: each title is made up of eight weeks (units) of work so your child can complete one unit each week during the summer vacation. The units are comprised of practice in English, Math, Science, and Social Studies. Engaging Arts and Crafts activities, as well as Comics and Fun Places to Go in Summer, are also included for added fun.

Your child will be delighted to have Canadian Curriculum SummerSmart as his or her summer learning buddy.

Your Partner in Education,
Popular Book Company (Canada) Limited

WEEK 1

English

- fill in the blanks to complete a poem
- colour a rainbow
- read and put pictures in order
- complete a word search

Mathematics

- do the counting
- do subtraction
- write the time
- draw clock hands

Science

- identify living and non-living things
- identify living things as plants or animals

Social Studies

- describe yourself

A. Complete the poem using the hints.

rain   sun
clouds   rainbow

It was a sunny day,

when big *clouds* got in the way.

The *rain* began to fall,

but the *sun* did not care at all.

It stayed out – the sky was blue.

Then a *rainbow* came shining through.

The colours were magic,

from what I could see.

Rain and sun shining,

how could it be?

B. Colour the rainbow using the hints.

red like an

orange like a

yellow like a

green like a

blue like a

purple like

C. **Write 1, 2, 3, and 4 to put the pictures in order to show how to make a rainbow.**

1. Stand with the sun behind you.

2. Hold the garden hose up on your side.

3. Spray water in the air.

4. A rainbow is formed.

D. Find and circle ◯ these words in the word search.

gold   pot   sky
clouds   rainbow   colours
magic   sunny

a	g	e	r	i	o	s	u	n	n	y	l
r	a	i	n	b	o	w	q	w	b	n	m
c	q	v	c	x	z	h	f	y	t	r	u
l	k	e	m	a	g	i	c	y	b	h	i
o	r	q	f	h	e	q	y				
u	d	j	h	q	e						
d	q	e	a	u						p	n
s	w	g	f					a	t	r	c
s	w	v				e	q	a	k	o
q	x				g	p	o	t	i	l
e	z			s	k	r	q	y	v	o
g			g	k	u	w	e	o	i	u
			g	y	i	g	o	l	d	r
			l	d	e	w	u	k	s

Some people think there is a pot of gold at the end of a rainbow.

9

A. Count how many children there are in each game. Then write the number in the circle.

1.

2.

3.

4.

5.

B. Colour the children's toys.

I have 3 balls, 3 spinning tops, and 1 robot. Please colour my toys green.

I have 1 ball, 5 spinning tops, and 2 robots. Please colour my toys red.

Tom   Sue

C. See how many candies Sue has. Then cross out ✗ the candies that she gives to her friends. Fill in the blanks.

1.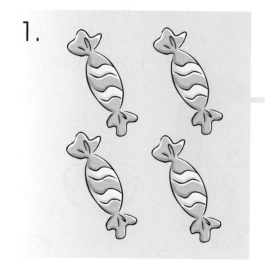

Sue has __4__ .

If she gives 3 🍬 to Ray, she will have __1__ 🍬 left.

2.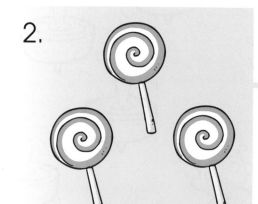

Sue has __3__ 🍭 .

If she gives 1 🍭 to Peter, she will have __2__ 🍭 left.

3.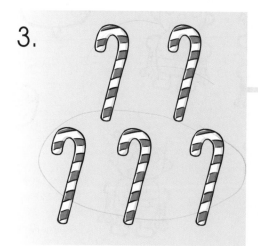

Sue has __5__ 🍬 .

If she gives 2 🍬 to Gloria, she will have __3__ 🍬 left.

D. Write or draw the clock hands to show the times.

1.   starts at _____ o'clock

finishes at
2 o'clock

2.

starts at _____ o'clock

stops sledding
at 1 o'clock

3.   starts at _____ o'clock

stops playing
at 6 o'clock

A. Do the matching.

Week

1

Science

Living Things

Non-living Things

B. Put the living things in two groups.

Plant

Animal

A. **Draw yourself in the box. Then write, circle ◯, and colour to describe yourself.**

Name: _____

Age: _____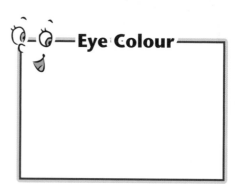

Hair Colour

Eye Colour

B. **Draw your face in the circle. Then describe more about yourself with the help of the given words.**

Food Items

bread

apple

ice cream

Animals

cat

dog

lion

Colours

red

yellow

green

My favourite food is _____.

My favourite animal is _____.

My favourite colour is _____.

English

- answer questions about a poem
- use ordinal numbers
- learn the number words
- solve riddles

Mathematics

- use position words
- count the number of objects
- learn about comparative words
- describe a picture with numbers and ordinal numbers

Science

- learn about the life cycle of a plant and a frog

Social Studies

- match responsibilities with places
- show your roles and responsibilities

A. Read the poem. Then answer the questions.

The Hopscotch Hop

Let's make a game for you and me.

You will see how much fun it can be.

We will draw some lines and numbers too,

using the colours red and blue.

Then hop from numbers one to nine.

When we are done,

we will start again!

1. What game are they playing?

   _____

2. What did they draw?

   _____ and _____

3. What colours did they use to draw?

   _____ and _____

B. Label each toy with the correct ordinal number.

third   tenth   seventh   fifth

fourth   first   sixth

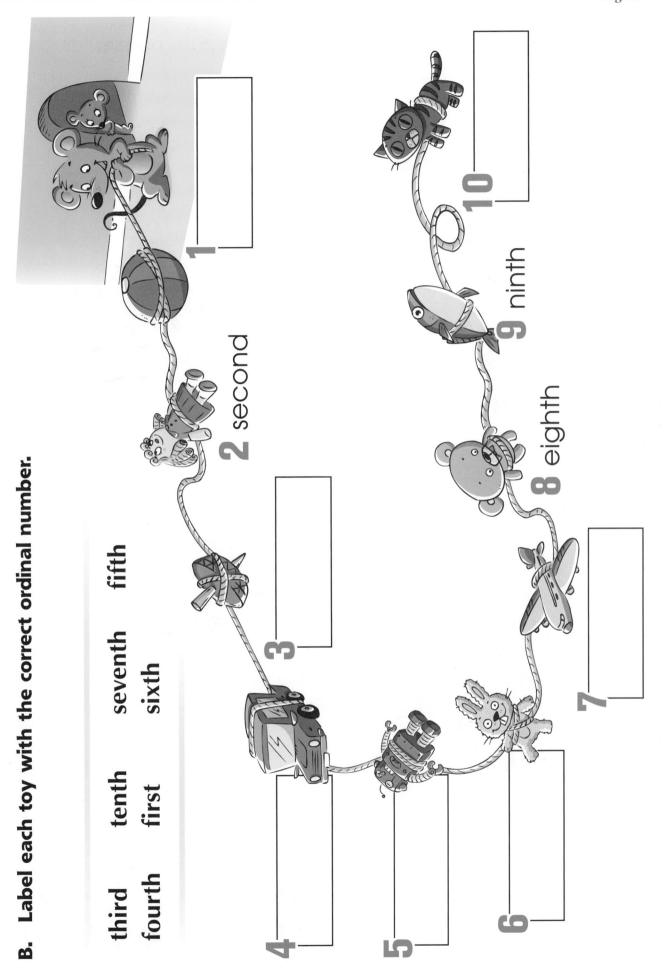

1

2 second

3

4

5

6

7

8 eighth

9 ninth

10

21

C. Follow the code to colour the hopscotch course.

brown like a
7

red like an
2

pink like a
8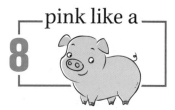

blue like a
9

orange like a
5

green like a
6

nine

eight

six

seven

five

three

four

two

one

yellow like the
1

purple like
3

black like a
4

D. Circle ◯ the correct pictures.

1. I have eight legs.

2. I have ten toes.

What Am I ?

3. I have two feet.

4. I have four paws.

A. Look at the picture. Circle ◯ the correct words.

1. The bee is **above / below** the basket.

2. The snail is **behind / under** the big flower.

3. The apples are **in front of / behind** the fairies.

4. The small flowers are **between / beside** the basket.

5. A fairy is waving at the butterfly with her **left / right** hand.

B. Count and write the numbers.

1. box   5
2. ball   4
3. robot   3
4. car   4
5. book   8
6. bear   2
7. doll   2
8. pencil   3
9. balloon   4
10. backpack   2

C. Colour the correct pictures to match the descriptions.

1. thicker

2. empty

3. longer

4.

taller

D. Circle ◯ the correct answers or write numbers to complete the sentences.

1.  /  /  / is on the eighth cart.

2. The purple cart is the   **fifth / sixth**   cart in line.

3. The   **green / blue**   cart is the fourth cart in line.

4. There are _____ carts between the two red carts.

5. There are _____ carts in all.

27

A. Write 1, 2, 3, and 4 to put the pictures in order to show the life cycle of a plant.

The Life Cycle of a Plant

B. Colour the arrows and trace the words to show the life cycle of a frog.

The **Life Cycle** of a **Frog**

egg

tadpole

frog

29

A. Match to show how responsibilities change with each place.

Responsibility

Place

- home
- school
- park

B. Draw yourself at home. Then circle ○ your roles and check ✔ your responsibilities.

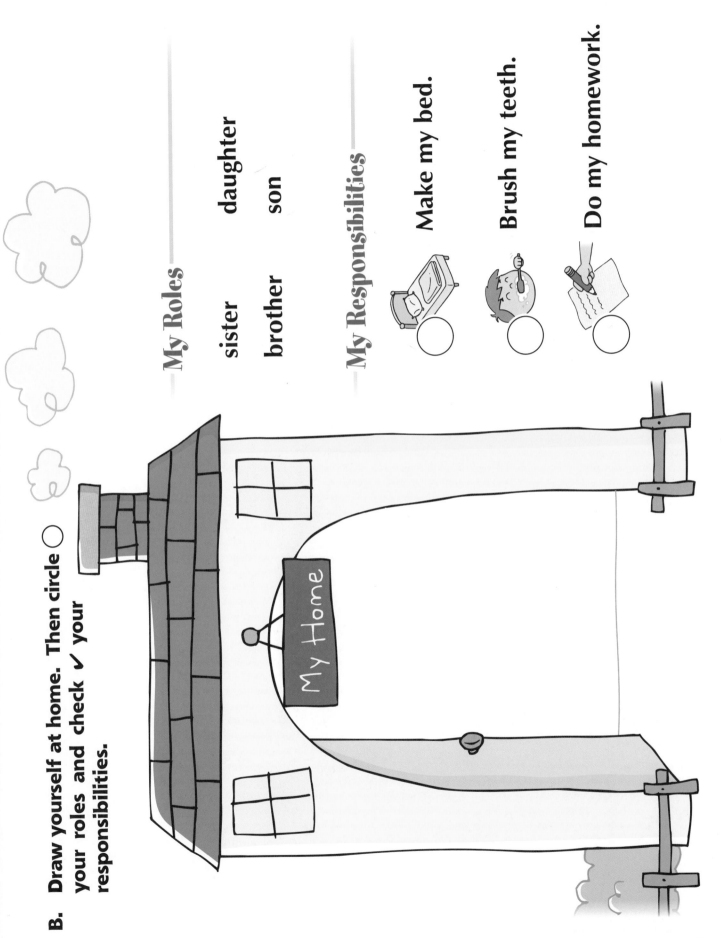

My Roles

sister   daughter

brother   son

My Responsibilities

Make my bed.

Brush my teeth.

Do my homework.

31

WEEK 3

English

- read a story and complete sentences
- follow instructions to draw pictures
- decode a message
- read to complete a maze

Mathematics

- put things in order
- learn about descriptive words
- complete a pictograph
- do the counting

Science

- sort animals by the places they live
- identify the homes of animals

Social Studies

- identify children showing respect to others and their surroundings

A. Read the story. Then circle ◯ the correct words to complete the sentences.

The Birthday Queen

On my birthday, I feel like a queen.

My dad makes a special breakfast, just for me.

Later, I have a party with my friends.

We eat cake and play games.

Then I open my gifts.

I have fun all day long.

I love my birthday!

1. This story is about a **girl / boy** .

2. Her dad makes her a special **breakfast / lunch** .

3. She receives many **games / gifts** .

4. At the party, they **swim / eat** .

B. Read, draw, and colour.

- Draw a crown  on the girl's head.

- Draw six candles on the cake.

- Draw a party hat on the boy's head.

C. Meg got a gift that made her birthday wish come true. Use the code to see what Meg wished for. Then colour her gift.

1	2	3	4	5	6	7	8	9	10	11	12	13
A	B	C	D	E	F	G	H	I	J	K	L	M

14	15	16	17	18	19	20	21	22	23	24	25	26
N	O	P	Q	R	S	T	U	V	W	X	Y	Z

Week

3

To: Meg

___ ___ ___   ___ ___ ___ ___ ___ ___
13   5   7   23   9   19   8   5   4

___ ___ ___ ___   ___ ___ ___ ___ ___
 6 15 18   1   16 21 16 16 25

HAPPY BIRTHDAY

English

D. Draw lines to match the clues with the gifts.

You can draw with it.

You can play with it.

You can wear it.

You can read it.

A. Put the things in order. Write the letters on the lines.

1.

small to big:

_____ , _____ , _____

2.

thick to thin:

_____ , _____ , _____

3.

light to heavy:

_____ , _____ , _____

4.

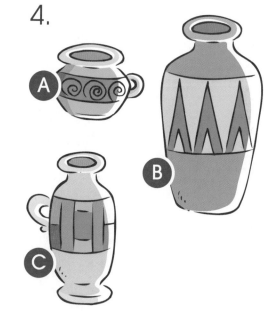

tall to short:

_____ , _____ , _____

B. **Look at the recipe. Colour the cups to show the amount of juice needed to make fruit punch.**

Recipe

orange juice (3 cups)

pineapple juice (4 cups)

kiwi juice (2 cups)

apple juice (6 cups)

39

C. Circle  **the things Tom has.**

3 marbles

2 flowers

4 lollipops

5 crayons

D. Read what the children say and colour their hats or caps. Then count and write the numbers.

1.

I have 3 blue hats and 1 red hat.

Total

_____ hats

2.

I have 2 yellow caps, 3 green caps, and 1 red cap.

Total

_____ caps

41

A. Sort the animals by writing the letters in the correct boxes.

Where Animals Live

On Land

In Water

On Land and in Water

Some animals live on land, some live in water, and some can live both on land and in water.

B. Check ✔ the animals that are in the correct homes and put a cross ✘ for the ones that are not.

A. Draw a happy face 😊 **in the circle if the children are showing respect to others.**

B. Circle ○ the correct words to show how people respect their surroundings.

At school

Here you go!

Hide / Share things.

In a library

Speak **loudly / quietly** .

At a park

Do / Do not litter.

Arts & Crafts
- make flowers and a flowerpot

Comics
- The Circus Clown

Fun Places to Go in Summer
- Santa's Village

Flower Family

Materials:

- juice container
- construction paper
- 1 green foam sheet
- bright-coloured foam sheets
- Popsicle sticks (one for each member of your family)
- glue
- marbles
- scissors

Directions:

1. Glue construction paper to juice container.

2. Fill container halfway with marbles.

3. Trace flowers onto bright-coloured foam sheets and cut them out (one for each member of your family).

4. Glue flowers to Popsicle sticks.

5. Trace leaves on green foam sheet and cut them out.

6. Glue leaves to Popsicle "stems".

7. "Plant" flowers in container.

The Circus Clown

Tom went to the circus. He had a lot of fun. After the show, he saw a boy sitting outside the tent. He looked unhappy. Tom asked him why.

The boy's name was Jake. His parents were tightrope walkers.

They want me to become a tightrope walker. But I want to be a clown.

Tom and Jake watched all the acts together.

Chips

I'd prefer a bag of chips!

Then they visited Jake's mom and dad.

You'll be doing this soon, Jake!

The boys walked past the grumpy clown. They walked just like him.

The ringmaster saw the boys and laughed. He told them that they could act as real clowns in the show that evening.

That's great!

Tom and Jake dressed up as clowns. They laughed at their big shoes and red noses.

Tom did cartwheels, while Jake walked on his hands.

Jake could keep seven hoops twirling. Tom just kept dropping them.

It was time for the boys' part in the show.

They threw water at the grumpy clown.

The audience pointed and laughed.

Son, I think you should be a clown, not a tightrope walker.

Hurray!

The End

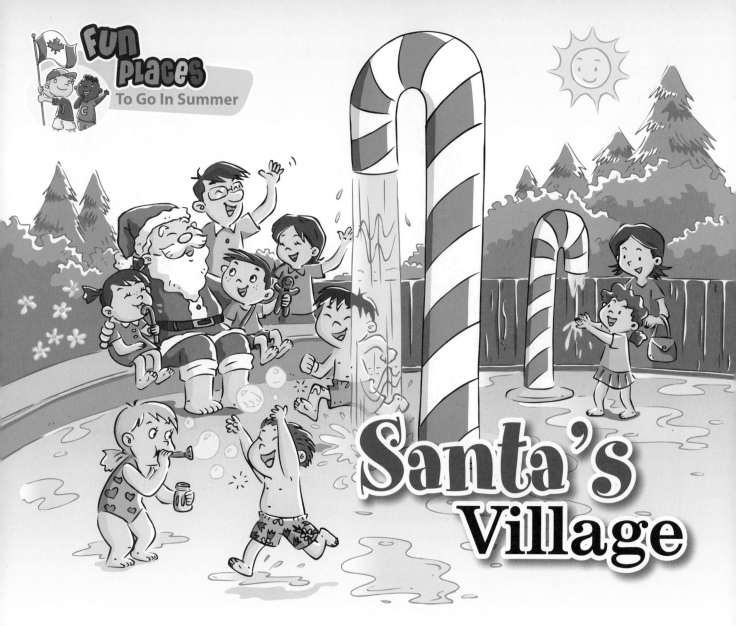

Santa's Village

Have you ever thought of meeting Santa in the summer? Go to Santa's Village, Santa's summer home in Bracebridge, Ontario.

After greeting Santa and taking photos with him, you can try some gingerbread cookies at Mrs. Claus's bakery, and feed Santa's reindeer. Then, make a wish at Santa's Wishing Well, ride on Santa's Express Train, enjoy the great view on the Christmas Ball Ferris Wheel, and take a boat ride down the beautiful Muskoka River. The water play area is also a great place to get wet and have fun.

Ho! Ho! Ho! Santa's Village is sure to have something for you!

English

- read a story and find specific words
- complete a crossword puzzle
- match opposite words
- identify words that rhyme

Mathematics

- identify shapes and solids
- complete patterns
- put things in pairs

Science

- identify things that absorb water
- identify things that float or sink

Social Studies

- identify things that belong to nature
- identify people who treat nature correctly

A. Read the story. Circle ◯ the Dd words with a  **. Circle ◯ the Ww words with a ⬭ .**

On the Beach

Sam and Sara went to

the ⬭ one ☀ day.

They wanted to make a 🏰 in the sand.

Sam filled his 🪣 with cold water.

Sara dumped it on the dry 🏖 .

They made tall and short 🏰 walls.

Sam made a ⊞ up high as a lookout.

Sara made a secret ⊞ down low.

They used ✕ and 🐚 to decorate.

B. Look at the picture clues and complete the crossword puzzle.

C. Look at the words and pictures. Then match the opposites.

Opposites

big   small

dry   cold

hot   sunny

cloudy   wet

long   short

English

D. Say what each picture is. Then circle ◯ the word that rhymes with it.

sad

mad
dog
six

pan

fan
bug
net

bat

pen
hat
box

cap

jet
map
cat

bag

key
bed
tag

A. Colour the correct shapes in each group.

B. Follow the pattern to draw the next 2 pictures in each group.

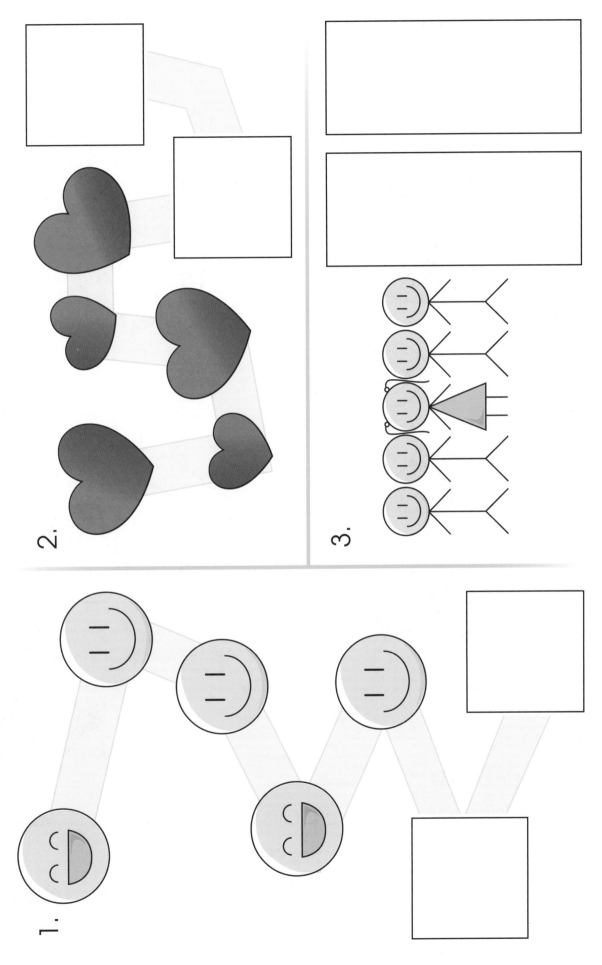

1.

2.

3.

C. The items are in pairs. Circle ◯ every 2 items and write the numbers to complete what the girl says.

There are _____ pairs of slippers, _____ pairs of mittens, and _____ pairs of socks.

D. Draw lines to match the gift boxes with the gifts.

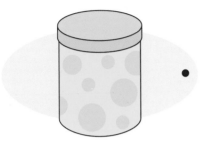 •

•

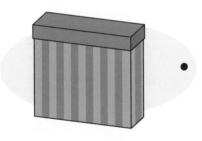 •

•

 •

•

 •

•

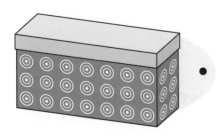 •

•

A. Draw lines to bring the things that absorb water to the spilled water.

Things that Absorb Water

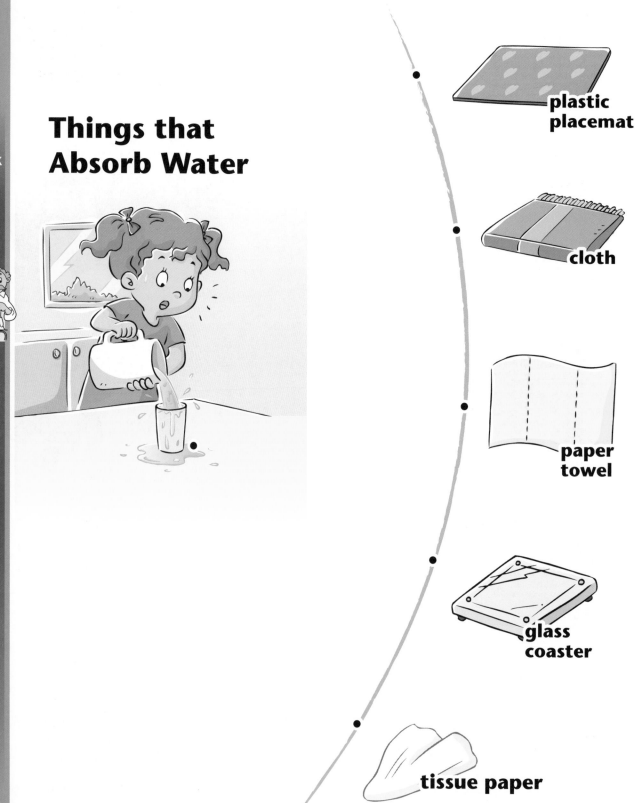

plastic placemat

cloth

paper towel

glass coaster

tissue paper

B. Cross out **x** the things in the wrong places.

Float

Sink

A. Colour the things that belong to nature. Then colour the paths to bring them to nature.

B. Check ✔ if the people treat nature correctly.

English

- read a letter and identify true sentences
- complete a word search
- read, draw, and colour a summer scene
- sort objects

Mathematics

- compare capacity of containers
- count and add
- count and subtract

Science

- identify things that flow
- choose suitable materials for items

Social Studies

- identify who does what in your community
- complete paragraphs about recycling rules

A. Read the letter. Then check ✔ the true sentences.

Dear Mom and Dad,

I am having fun with Lee and her family. During the day, we swim at the lake, go fishing, and play ball games. At night, we have a campfire. Then we go in the tent to play cards. I like camping.

See you on Friday.

Love,
Wayne

Camping Fun

1. Wayne goes camping with his mom and dad. _____

2. Wayne swims at the lake. _____

3. Lee goes camping with Wayne. _____

4. They play ball games in the tent. _____

5. Wayne will go home on Friday. _____

6. Wayne likes camping. _____

B. Find the words in bold in the word search. Colour the words with the specified colours.

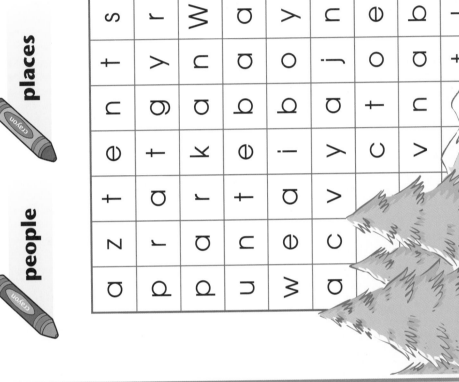

people (crayon) places (crayon) things (crayon)

a	z	t	e	n	t	s	a	b	y
p	r	a	t	g	y	r	e	h	m
p	a	r	k	a	n	w	a	a	t
u	n	t	e	b	a	a	v	q	i
w	e	a	v	i	b	o	y	s	e
a	c	v	y	c	t	o	e	m	s
				v	n	a	b	v	t	a
					t	l	a	k	e
						n	a	m

- The **lake** is big.
- The **tent** is new.
- **Wayne** likes to camp.
- The **trees** are tall.
- A **park** is nearby.
- The **boys** like to fish.

C. Read, draw, and colour.

Draw a tent under the tree.

Draw a girl near the tent.

Draw a boy flying a kite .

English

D. Read the sentences. Help Wayne put his things back in the drawers by drawing the pictures and writing the words in the correct places.

Put the...

-  cap in the third drawer.

-  sunglasses in the first drawer.

-  shorts in the fourth drawer.

-  T-shirt in the second drawer.

-  towel in the fifth drawer.

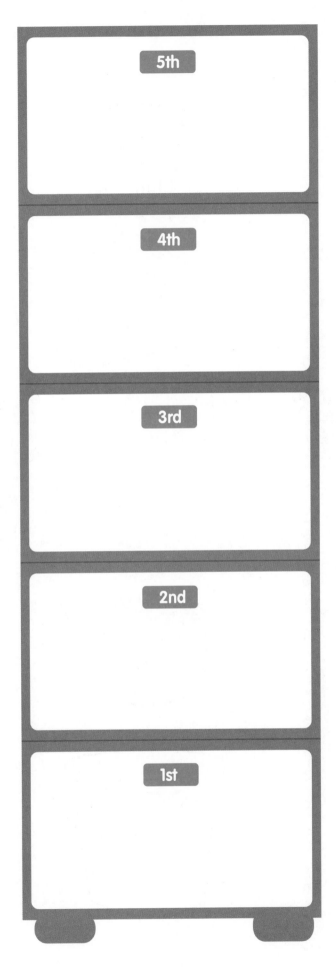

73

A. Colour the container that can hold more in each pair.

1.

Yogourt

Ice cream

2.

3.

My water bottle can hold more than a juice box.

JUICE

4.

B. See how full each container is. Draw lines to match the containers with the correct words.

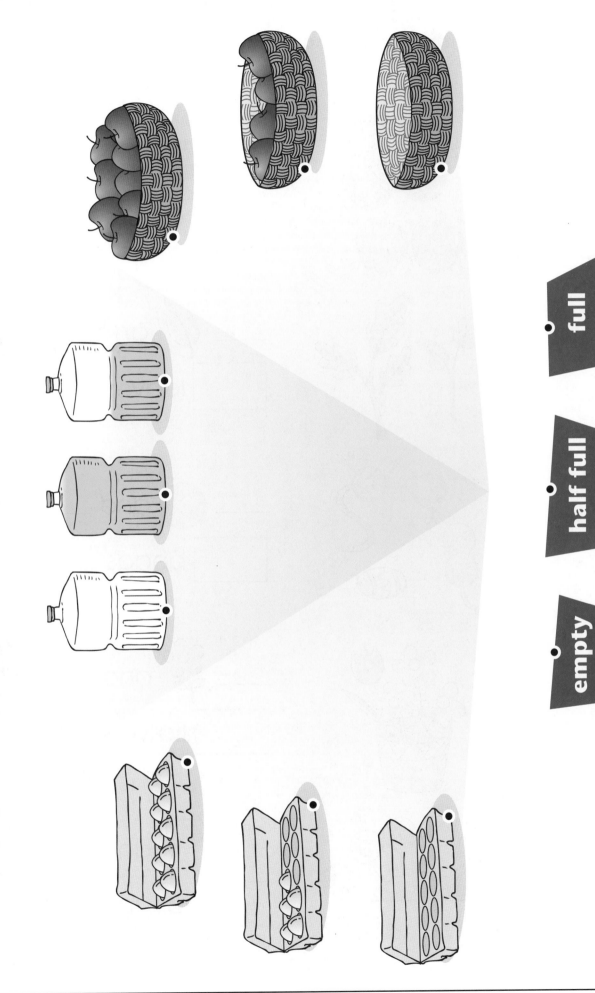

full

half full

empty

Week

6

Mathematics

C. Count the objects and solve the problems.

1.    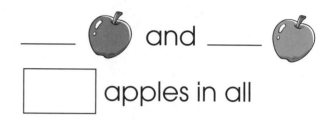

_____ 🍎 and _____ 🍎

[ ] apples in all

2.    

_____ 🍃 and _____ 🍃

[ ] leaves in all

3. 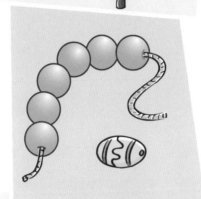   

_____ ⚪ and _____ 🥚

[ ] beads in all

4.    

_____ 🌸 and _____ 🌷

[ ] flowers in all

5.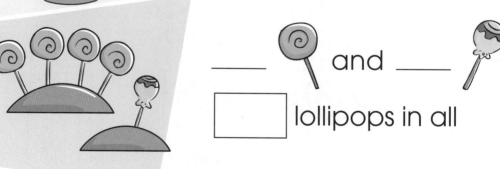

_____ 🍭 and _____ 🍭

[ ] lollipops in all

D. Count the objects and write the numbers.

1.

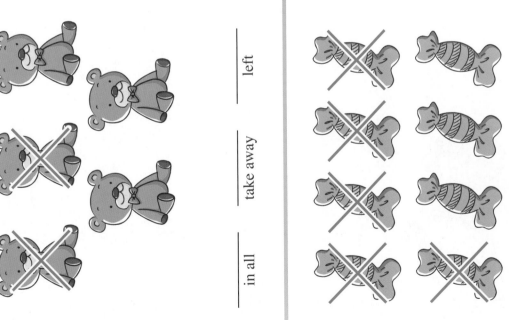

_____ in all   take away _____   _____ left

2.

_____ in all   take away _____   _____ left

3.

_____ in all   take away _____   _____ left

4.

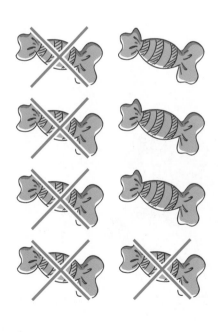

_____ in all   take away _____   _____ left

A. **Identify the things that can get through the funnel. Write the letters on the lines. Then circle ◯ the correct word.**

Anything that can get through the funnel can **float / flow** .

B. Circle ⭕ the best material to make each object.

1.

glass

wood

rubber

2.

leather

metal

cloth

3.

metal

glass

paper

4.

wood

leather

cardboard

5.

plastic

metal

wood

A. Circle ◯ to show who provides each service in your community.

1.

bus driver

doctor

teacher

2.

principal

caretaker

plumber

3.

librarian

police officer

plumber

4.

crossing guard

doctor

firefighter

5.

mail carrier

coach

librarian

Week **6**

Social Studies

B. **Fill in the blanks to complete the paragraphs. Then draw lines to bring the correct materials to the recycling box.**

We can also help our community by recycling.

Recycling Rules!

save   new
plastic

Recycling old materials means using them to make

_____ things. In this way, we can _____

resources and the energy used to make them.

Some materials that we can recycle are

paper, _____ , and glass.

English

- read a story and put events in order
- complete a word search
- write correct words
- use position words

Mathematics

- identify Canadian coins
- learn the value of coins
- measure with correct tools
- describe probability

Science

- identify things that keep sheets of paper together
- learn what wheels are for

Social Studies

- colour and draw places on a map
- show a path on a map

* The Canadian penny is no longer in circulation. It is used in the unit to show money amounts to the cent.

A. **Read the story. Write 1, 2, 3, and 4 to put the pictures in order.**

Picnic Time

Jill and Ken go to the park for a picnic.

They play on the swing and the slide until lunchtime.

Then Ken and Jill sit on a blanket under a tree.

They drink juice and eat sandwiches.

After lunch, they fly their kite.

B. **Find and circle ◯ these words in the word search.**

park   picnic   swing   slide   blanket
lunchtime   sandwiches   kite

l	u	n	c	h	t	i	m	e	v	n	a
k	n	r	n	z	b	k	i	t	e	l	s
e	s	m	r	l	e	p	s	n	u	k	i
i	l	b	l	a	n	k	e	t	n	s	e
s	i	b	e	g	s	q	t	b	y	t	m
a	d	q	e	b	w	q	y	d	w	c	o
n	e	b	a	q	i	b	j	i	l	h	h
d	n	q	g	h	n	t	j	w	e	q	y
w	h	a	h	v	g	z	r	o	t	k	c
i	p	i	c	n	i	c	v	o	y	e	a
c	b	n	k	b					h	e	n
h	l	p	y	n							
e	h	a	u	e							
s	l	r	j	g							
b	n	k	b	q							
q	l	r	n	g							

85

C. Look at each picture and read the words. Cross out ✗ the letter that is wrong in each word. Then write the correct words on the lines.

A b a l d

B b u n

C d o t

D l u c k

E n a i l

F s a n g

G f r e e

H m a t h

I a n d

 **Correct Words**

A ___ ___ ___

B ___ ___ ___

C ___ ___ ___

D ___ ___ ___

E ___ ___ ___ ___

F ___ ___ ___

G ___ ___ ___

H ___ ___ ___

I ___ ___ ___

D. Read the sentences below to identify the children in the picture. Write the names in the boxes.

John is **behind** the bench.

Tim is **on** the bench.

Bill is **beside** the tree.

Joe is **between** the sandcastles.

Ivy is **under** the umbrella.

Bob is playing **in** the sand.

A. Write the value of each coin. Then check ✔ the coins to show the amount in each group.

1. **Value**

penny

_____ ¢

dime

_____ ¢

nickel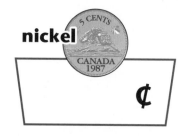

_____ ¢

2. **3¢**

3. **6¢**

4. **4¢**

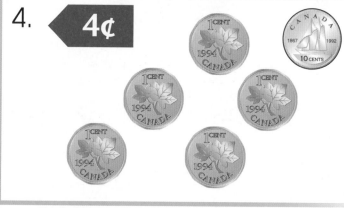

5. **7¢**

Mathematics

B. Count each type of coin in each piggy bank. Write the numbers in the boxes.

1.

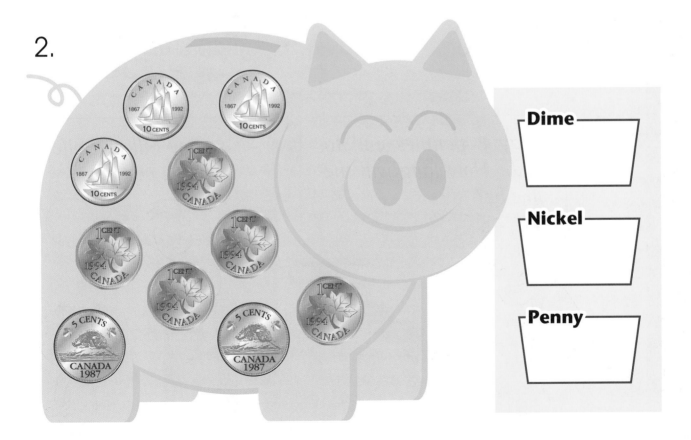

Dime

Nickel

Penny

2.

Dime

Nickel

Penny

C. Choose the correct tools to find the measurements. Write the letters in the circles.

Measuring Tools

1.

How heavy is a penny?

2.

How long does it take to stack 15 pennies?

3.

I lay 8 pennies end to end. How long will the line be?

4.

How tall is a pile of 30 pennies?

D. Look at the pictures. Write whether they are "likely" or "unlikely" to occur.

1. _____

2. _____

3. _____

4. _____

5. _____

6. _____

7. _____

A. Colour the things that can keep the sheets of paper together.

Please help me find the things that can keep my sheets of paper together.

B. **Write the letters to show what the things with wheels are mainly designed for.**

Functions

A for fun   **B** for moving things   **C** for getting around

1.

2.

3.

4.

5.

6.

A. Look at the map. Then colour and draw.

Lucy's Neighbourhood

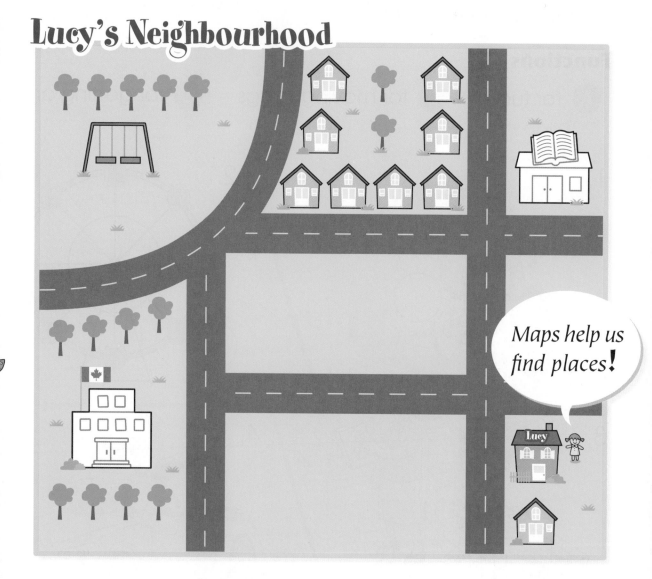

1. Colour the library blue and the school yellow.

2. Draw the following on the map.

- 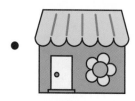 The flower shop is to the left of Lucy's house.

-  The cake shop is near the park.

To the Park

1. Go up.

2. Turn right and go down.

3. Turn left and go to the park!

Have Fun!

B. Draw yourself in the circle. Follow the instructions to draw lines on the map to show the path to the park.

Park

95

Arts & Crafts

• create a picture using leaves

Comics

• Sunny Farm

Fun Places to Go in Summer

• Downtown Toronto

My dad

My Mom

Leaf People

Materials: • markers • leaves • glue • crayons
• construction paper of various colours

Directions:

1. Find some leaves of different shapes, sizes, and colours.

2. Look at the leaves. Find a leaf that reminds you of a person.

3. Glue it to a piece of construction paper.

4. Draw arms, legs (head, if necessary), and add other details.

99

Sunny Farm

Lots of children visited Sunny Farm. They liked to feed the llamas and the goats.

But the work on the farm was becoming too hard for the old farmer.

Children stopped visiting it. And the farmer had no money to fix the mess.

Soon, Sunny Farm was a mess.

One day, a boy climbed onto the old roof.

Suddenly, the boy fell down. Two llamas quickly helped the boy.

Another llama fetched the farmer.

The boy's mother and father thanked the llamas for saving their son.

This is a story for the newspaper...

101

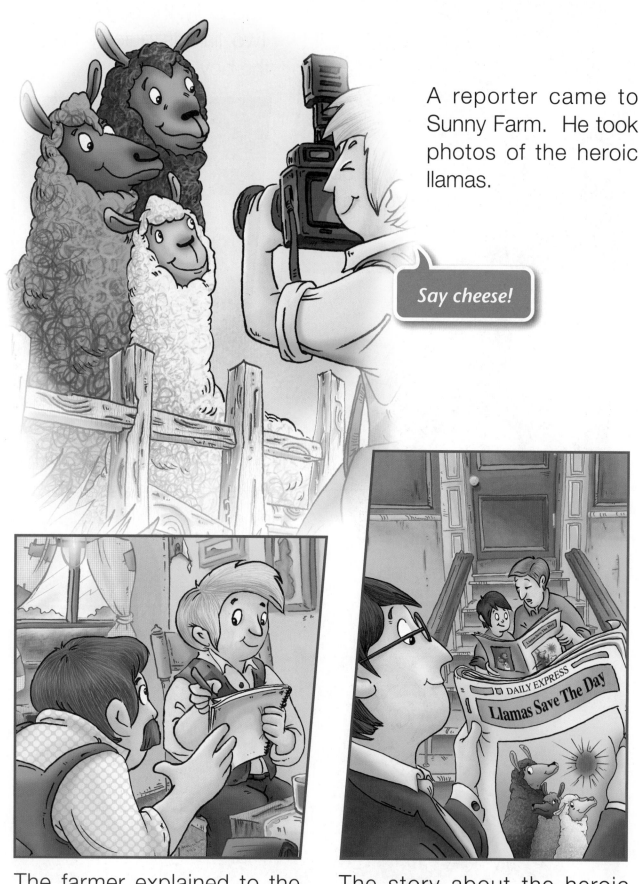

A reporter came to Sunny Farm. He took photos of the heroic llamas.

Say cheese!

The farmer explained to the reporter why the farm was such a mess.

The story about the heroic llamas and the poor farmer was in the newspaper.

Many people came to help the farmer. They collected money to mend the roof.

Soon, children came to visit the clean farm again.

They pet the donkey and sat on the pony.

But everyone liked the heroic llamas best.

The End

Downtown Toronto

The best way to see downtown Toronto is to take a 90-minute tour on a "Hippo", a bright yellow, funny-looking bus with a purple hippo on it. What makes this bus so special? It is a bus that floats!

The bus takes you past famous Toronto landmarks, such as the CN Tower, Rogers Centre, and Toronto City Hall. A friendly tour guide will tell you about the history of Toronto and the famous places along the way. Then comes the highlight of the tour – splashing into Lake Ontario on a bus! What can be more fun than to see Toronto's waterfront while cruising on a bus?

You are sure to enjoy a little splash in the water this summer!

Answers
Grades K-1

Credits
Photos ("children" Gennadiy Poznyakov/123RF.com, "beach" Alexandr Ozerov/123RF.com)

ANSWERS

Week 1

English

A. clouds ; rain ; sun ; rainbow

B.

C.

D.
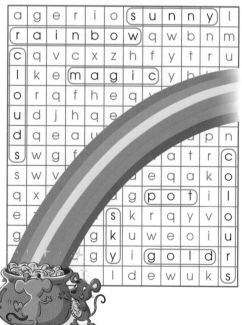

Mathematics

A. 1. 3   2. 1   3. 4
   4. 2   5. 5

B.

C. 1.
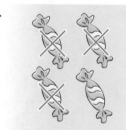
4 ; 1

2.

3 ; 2

3.
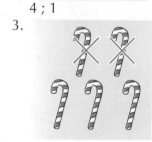
5 ; 3

D. 1. 1 ;

2. 11 ;

3. 4 ;

Science

A.

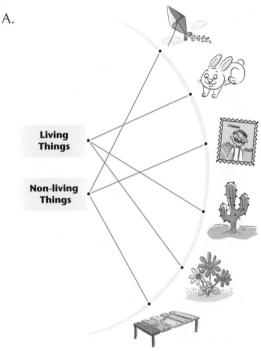

B. Plant: A, E, G, I
   Animal: B, C, D, F, H, J

Social Studies

A. (Individual drawing and answers)
B. (Individual drawing and answers)

Week 2

English

A. 1. hopscotch
   3. red ; blue

2. lines ; numbers

B. 1: first
   4: fourth
   6: sixth
   10: tenth

3: third
5: fifth
7: seventh

C.

D.

Mathematics

A. 1. above
   4. beside

2. under
5. left

3. behind

B. 1. 6
   4. 3
   7. 2
   10. 2

2. 4
5. 8
8. 7

3. 1
6. 2
9. 5

ANSWERS

C. 1.　　　　　2.

3.　　　　　4.

D. 1. 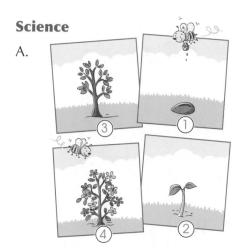　　　2. sixth　　　3. green

4. 5　　　5. 8

Science

A.

(3) (1) (4) (2)

B. (Colour the arrows and trace the words.)

Social Studies

A.

It looks good now.

I'm done!

Place
home
school
park

B. (Individual drawing and answers)

Week 3

English

A. 1. girl　　　　2. breakfast
　　3. gifts　　　4. eat

B.

C. MEG WISHED FOR A PUPPY

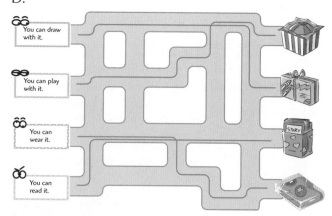

D.

You can draw with it.
You can play with it.
You can wear it.
You can read it.

Mathematics

A. 1. B ; A ; C　　　2. C ; A ; B
　　3. C ; B ; A　　　4. B ; C ; A

B.

C.
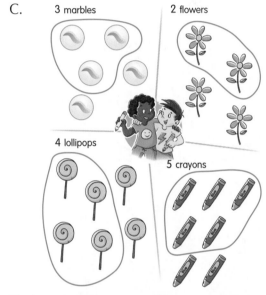

3 marbles   2 flowers
4 lollipops   5 crayons

D. 1.

4

2.
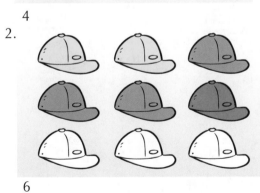
6

Science

A. On Land: A ; C   In Water: B ; F
   On Land and in Water: D ; E

B. 1. ✔   2. ✘   3. ✘
   4. ✔   5. ✔

Social Studies

A.

B. In a library: quietly
   At school: Share
   At a park: Do not

Week 5

English

A. Circle red: day ; dumped ; dry ; down ; decorate
   Circle blue: went ; wanted ; with ; water ; walls

B.

C.

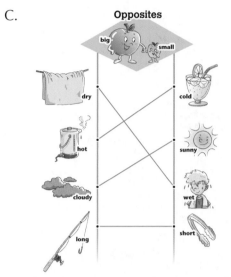

Opposites

big   small

dry — wet
hot — cold
cloudy — sunny
long — short

D.   bat: hat   pan: fan   sad: mad
     bag: tag   cap: map

Mathematics

A.

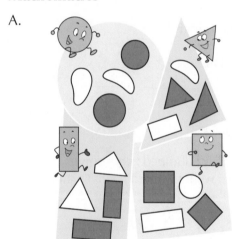

B.

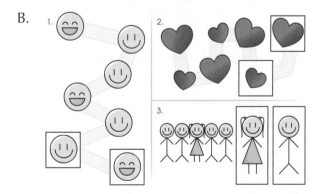

C.

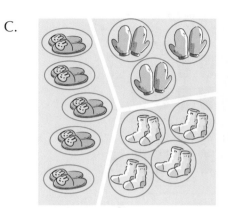

5 ; 3 ; 4

D.

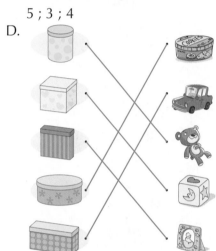

Science

A.

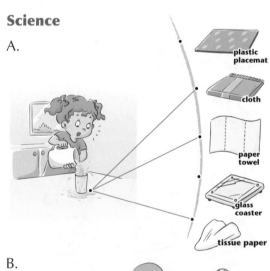

plastic placemat
cloth
paper towel
glass coaster
tissue paper

B.

Float

Sink

Social Studies

A.

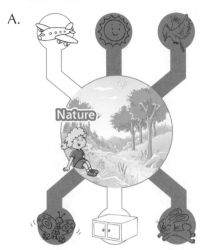

B. Check: C, E

Week 6

English

A. 1.   2. ✔   3. ✔
   4.   5. ✔   6. ✔

B.

a	z	t	e	n	t	s	a	b	y
p	r	a	t	g	y	r	e	h	m
p	a	r	k	a	n	W	a	a	t
u	n	t	e	b	a	a	v	q	r
w	e	a	i	b	o	y	s	i	e
a	c	v	y	a	j	n	k	p	s
		c	t	o	e	o	m	s	
		v	n	a	b	v	t	a	
			t	l	a	k	e		
				n	a	m			

C. (Individual drawing and colouring)

D.

Mathematics

A. 1.   2.   3.   4.

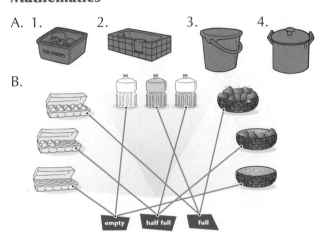

B.

C. 1. 4 ; 2 ; 6   2. 2 ; 3 ; 5
   3. 6 ; 1 ; 7   4. 3 ; 1 ; 4
   5. 4 ; 1 ; 5
D. 1. 5 ; 2 ; 3   2. 7 ; 3 ; 4
   3. 8 ; 5 ; 3   4. 4 ; 2 ; 2

Science

A. A ; B ; C ; H ; I
   flow
B. 1. wood   2. leather
   3. paper   4. wood
   5. metal

Social Studies

A. 1. bus driver   2. caretaker
   3. plumber   4. doctor
   5. mail carrier
B. new ; save ; plastic

111

Week 7

English

A.

B.

l	u	n	c	h	t	i	m	e	v	n	a
k	n	r	n	z	b	k	i	t	e	l	s
e	s	m	r	l	e	p	s	n	u	k	i
i	l	b	l	a	n	k	e	t	n	s	e
s	i	b	e	g	s	q	t	b	y	t	m
a	d	q	e	b	w	q	y	d	w	c	o
n	e	b	a	q	i	b	j	i	l	h	h
d	n	q	g	h	n	t	j	w	e	q	y
w	h	a	h	v	g	z	r	o	t	k	c
i	p	i	c	n	i	c	v	o	y	e	a
c	b	n	k	b				h	e	n	
h	l	p	y	n							
e	h	a	u	e							
s	l	r	j	g							
b	n	k	b	q							
q	l	r	n	g							

C. A: balx ; ball   B: xun ; sun
   C: dox ; dog   D: xuck ; duck
   E: xail ; pail   F: sanx ; sand
   G: xree ; tree   H: xath ; path
   I: anx ; ant

D. 1. John   2. Ivy   3. Tim
   4. Bob   5. Bill   6. Joe

Mathematics

A. 1. 1 ; 10 ; 5

   2.    3.

4.    5.

B. 1. 4 ; 1 ; 5   2. 3 ; 2 ; 5
C. 1. A   2. C
   3. B   4. B
D. 1. likely   2. likely   3. unlikely
   4. likely   5. likely   6. unlikely
   7. unlikely

Science

A. (Colour the following)

B. 1. A or C   2. A   3. B
   4. C   5. A or C   6. B

Social Studies

A.

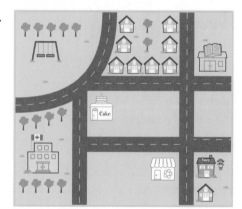

B. (Individual drawing of yourself)